Realistic Flowers
A hand-drawn coloring book

Queenie Wong

ISBN-13: 978-1533504210
ISBN-10: 1533504210
First published in United States in 2016
Illustrations by Queenie Wong
Wonger0050@yahoo.com.hk

List of 25 kinds of flowers below:

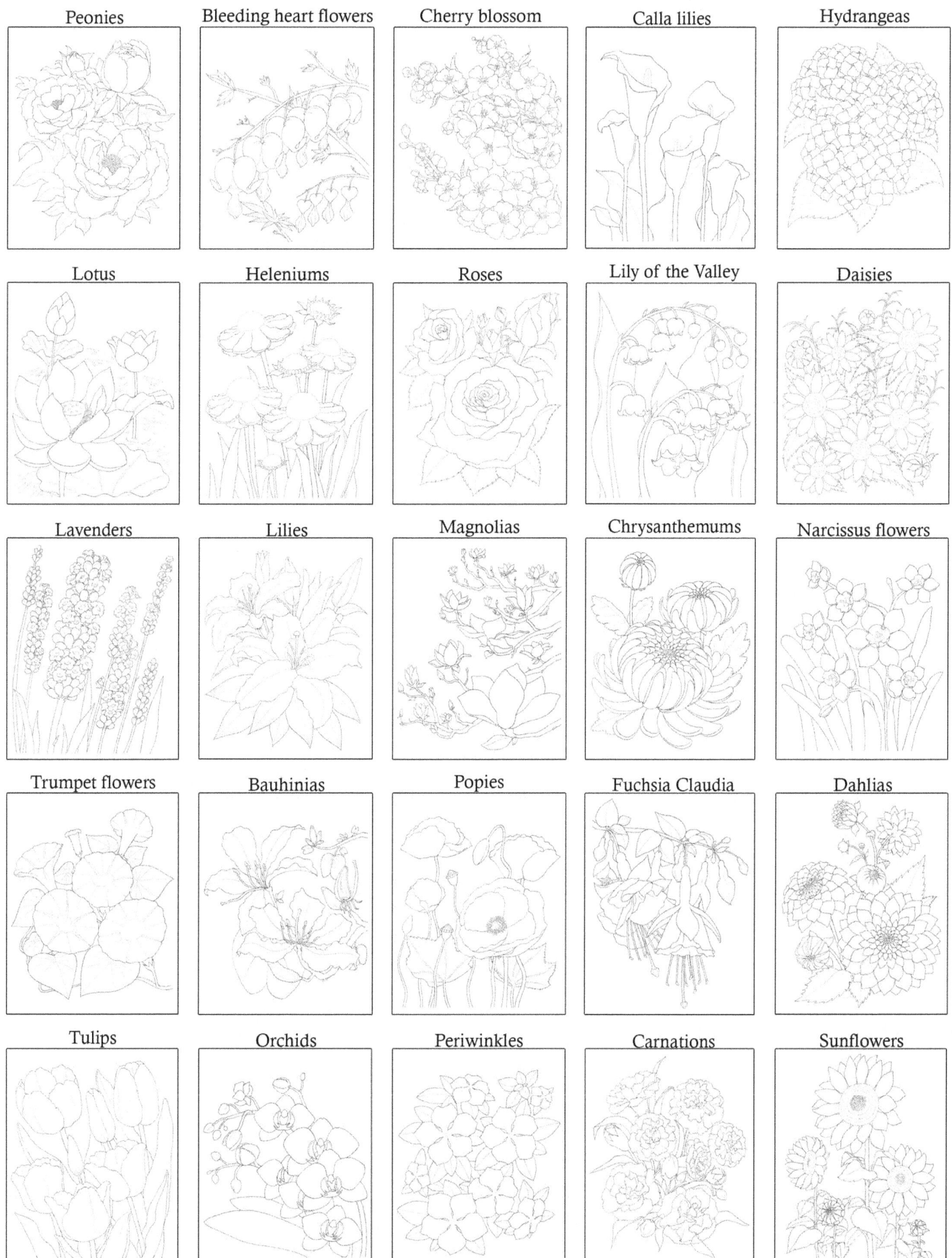

Peonies	Bleeding heart flowers	Cherry blossom	Calla lilies	Hydrangeas
Lotus	Heleniums	Roses	Lily of the Valley	Daisies
Lavenders	Lilies	Magnolias	Chrysanthemums	Narcissus flowers
Trumpet flowers	Bauhinias	Popies	Fuchsia Claudia	Dahlias
Tulips	Orchids	Periwinkles	Carnations	Sunflowers

Peonies

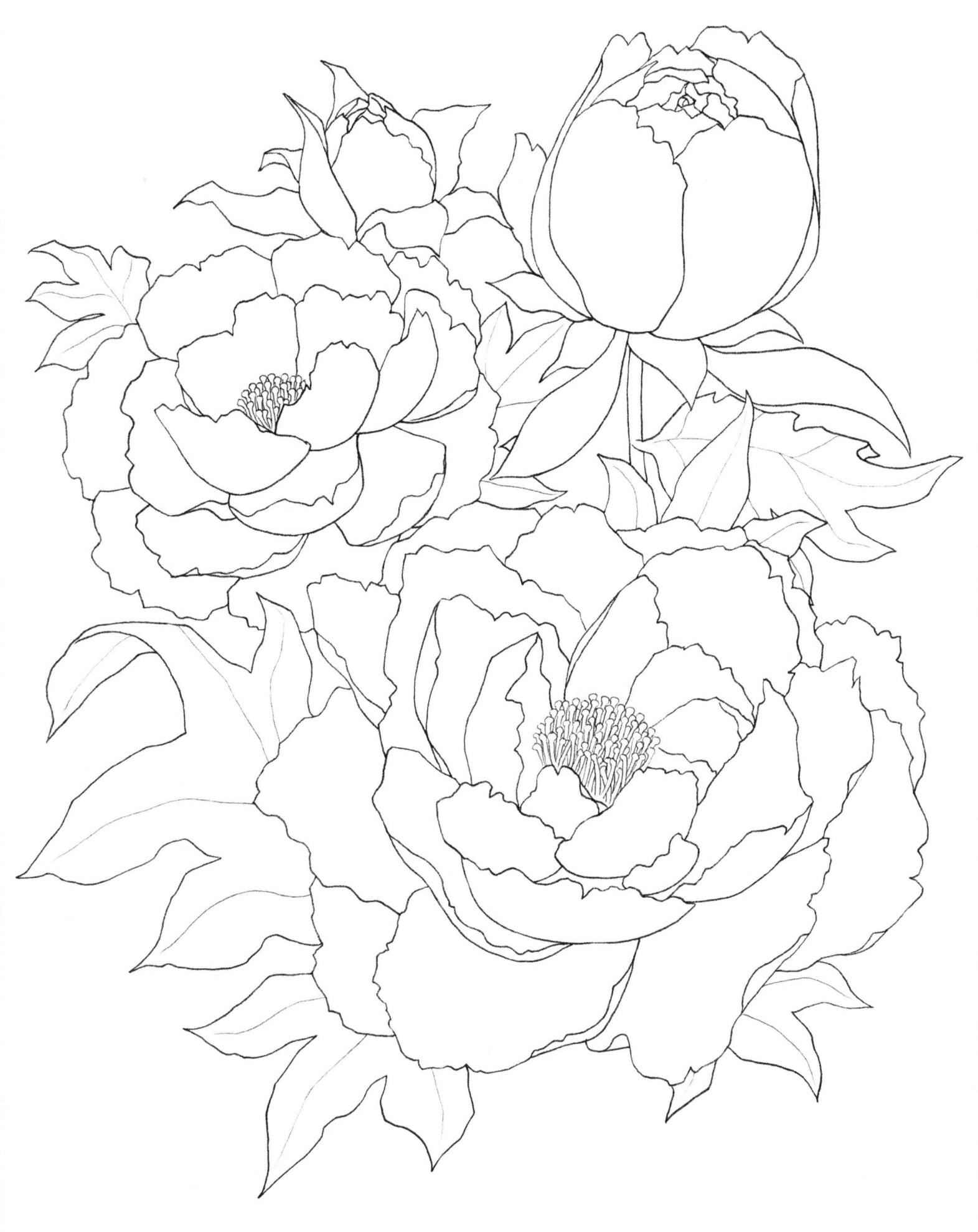

Bleeding heart flowers

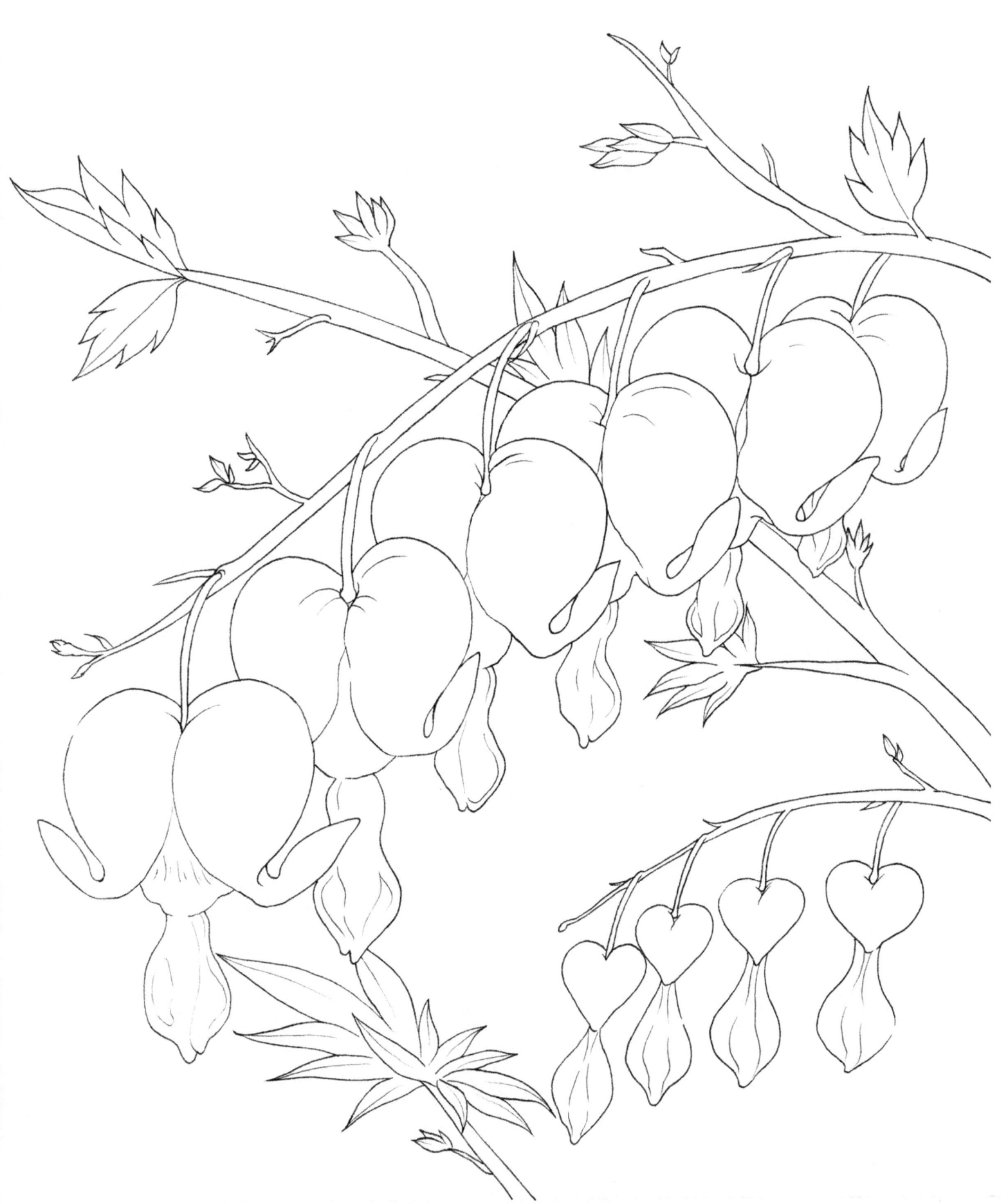

Cherry Blossom

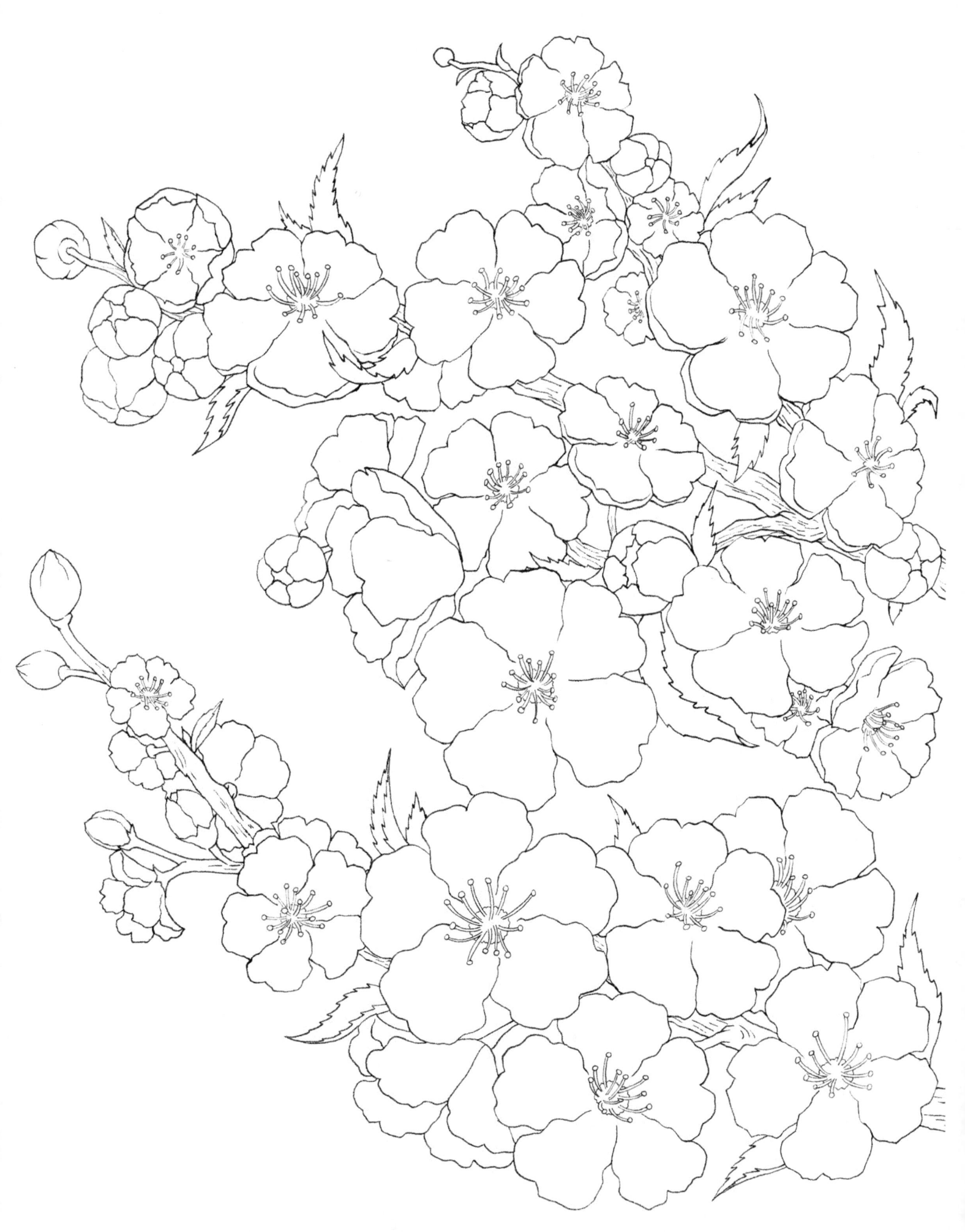

Calla lilies

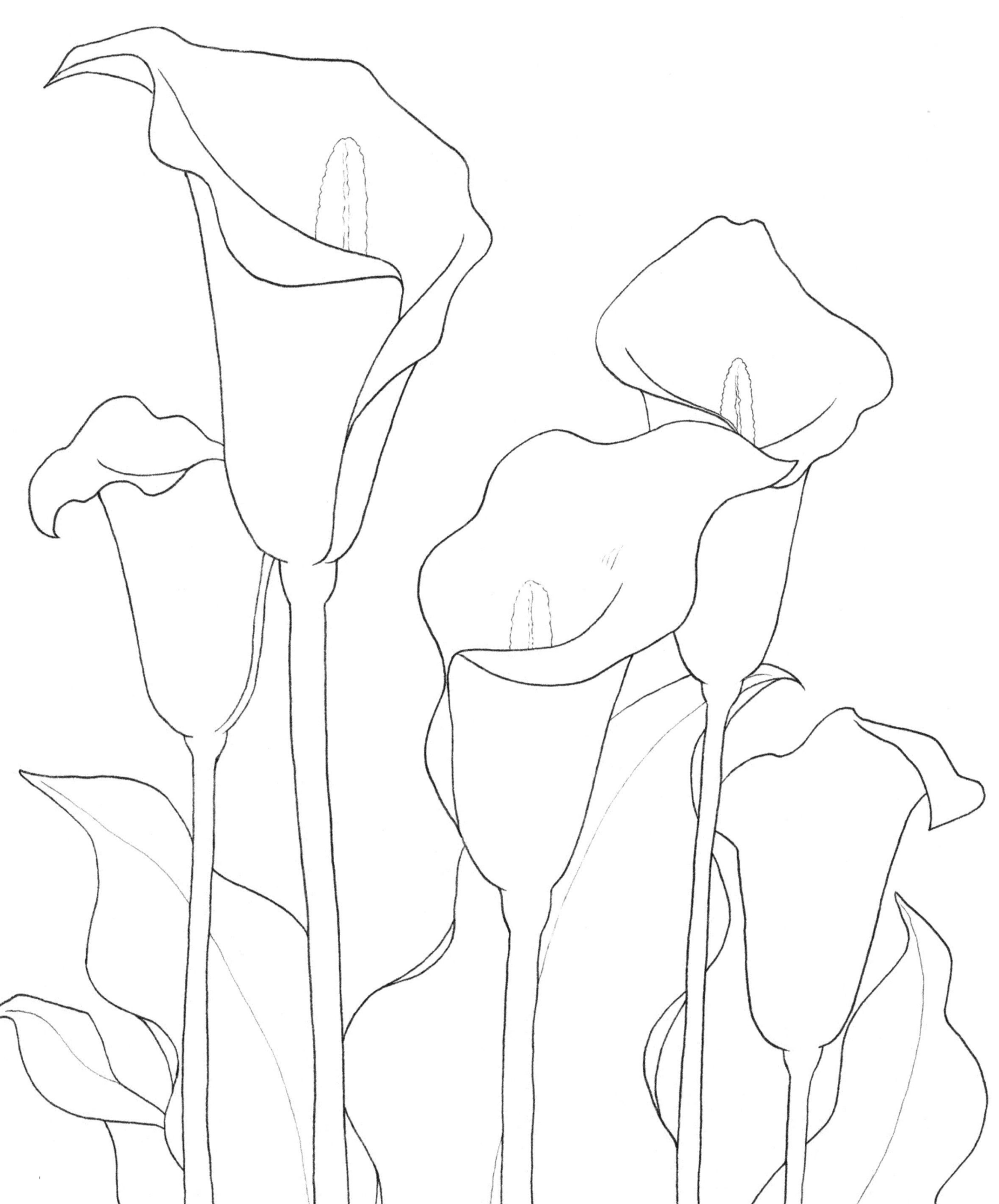

Hydrangeas

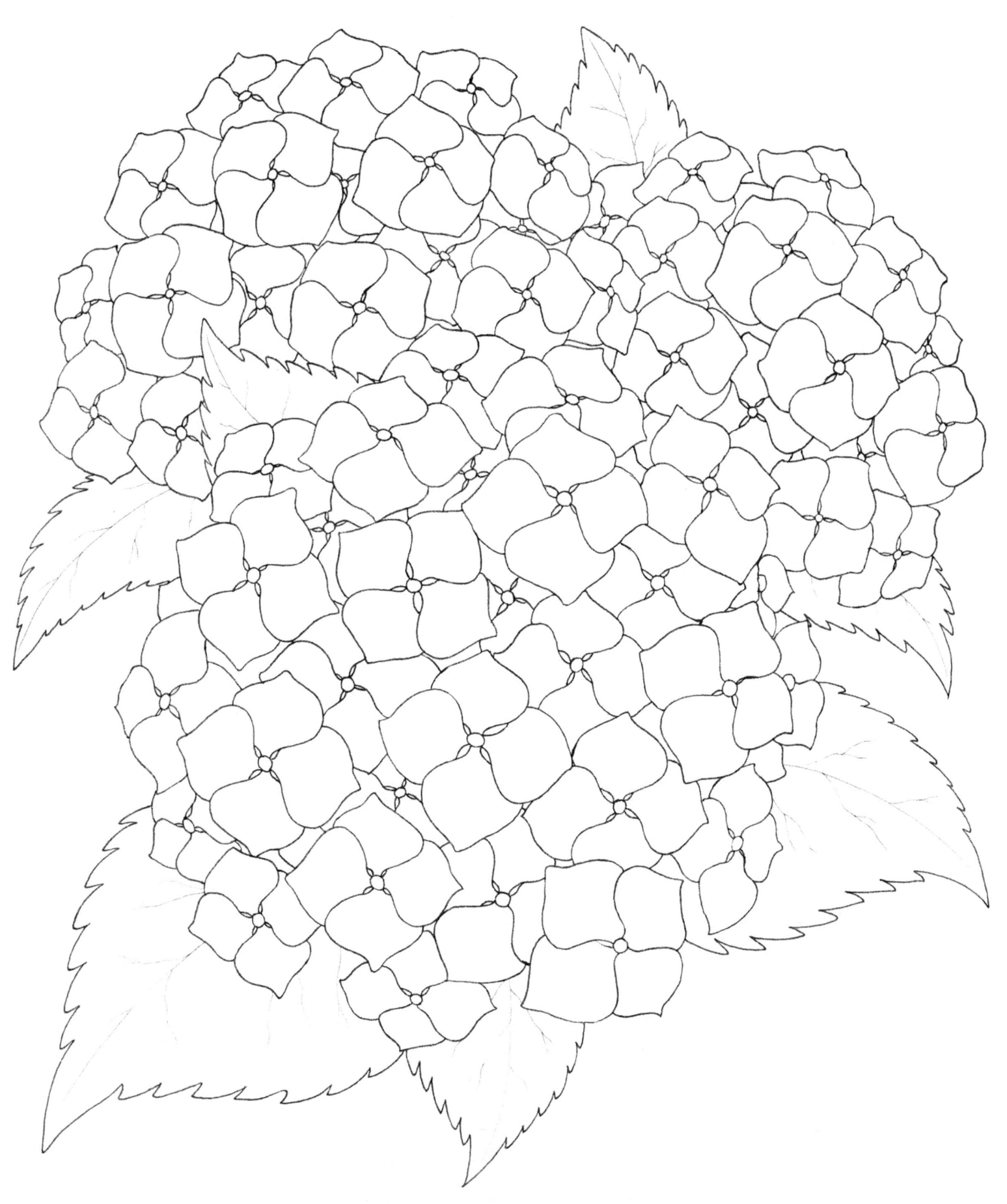

Lotus

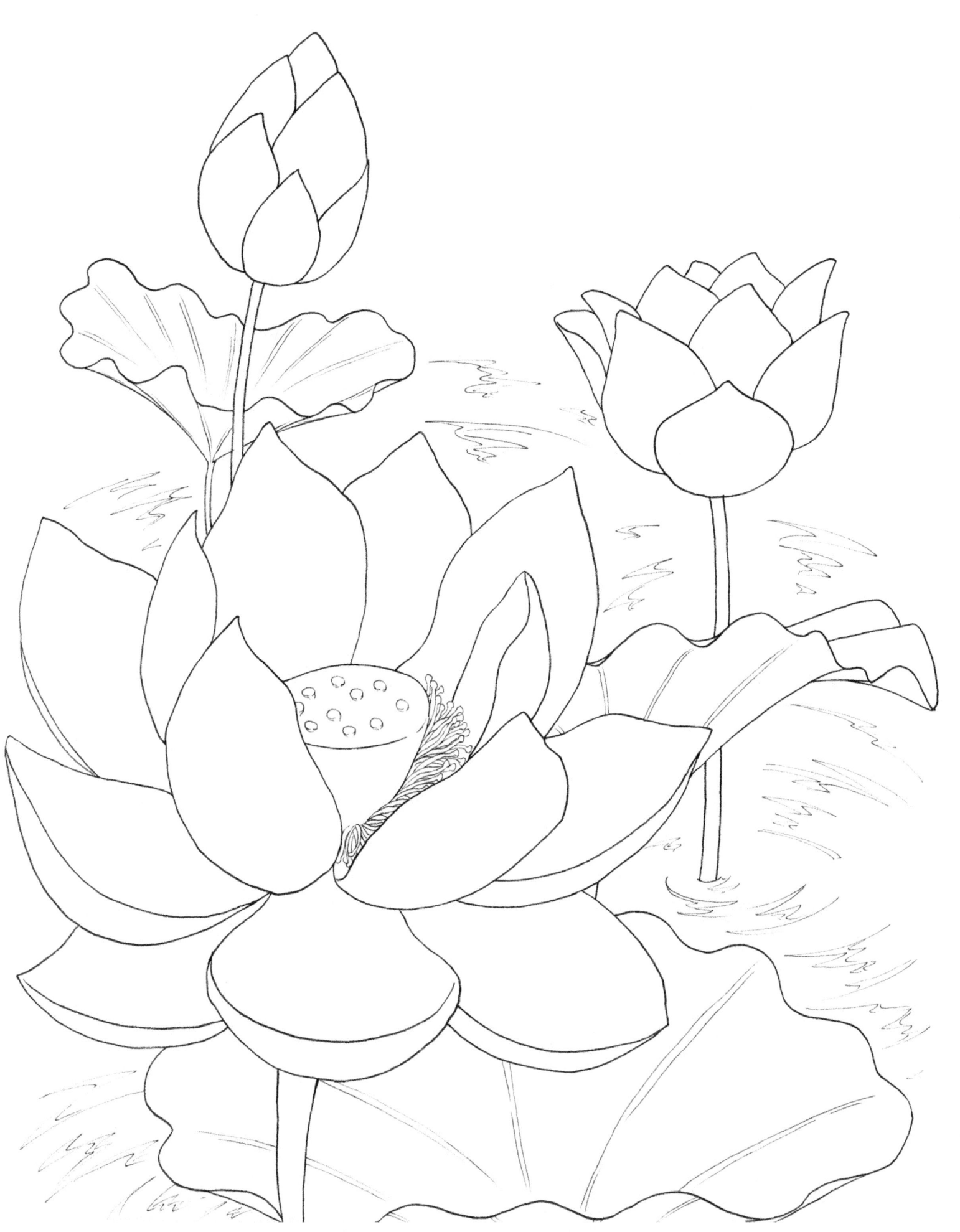

Heleniums

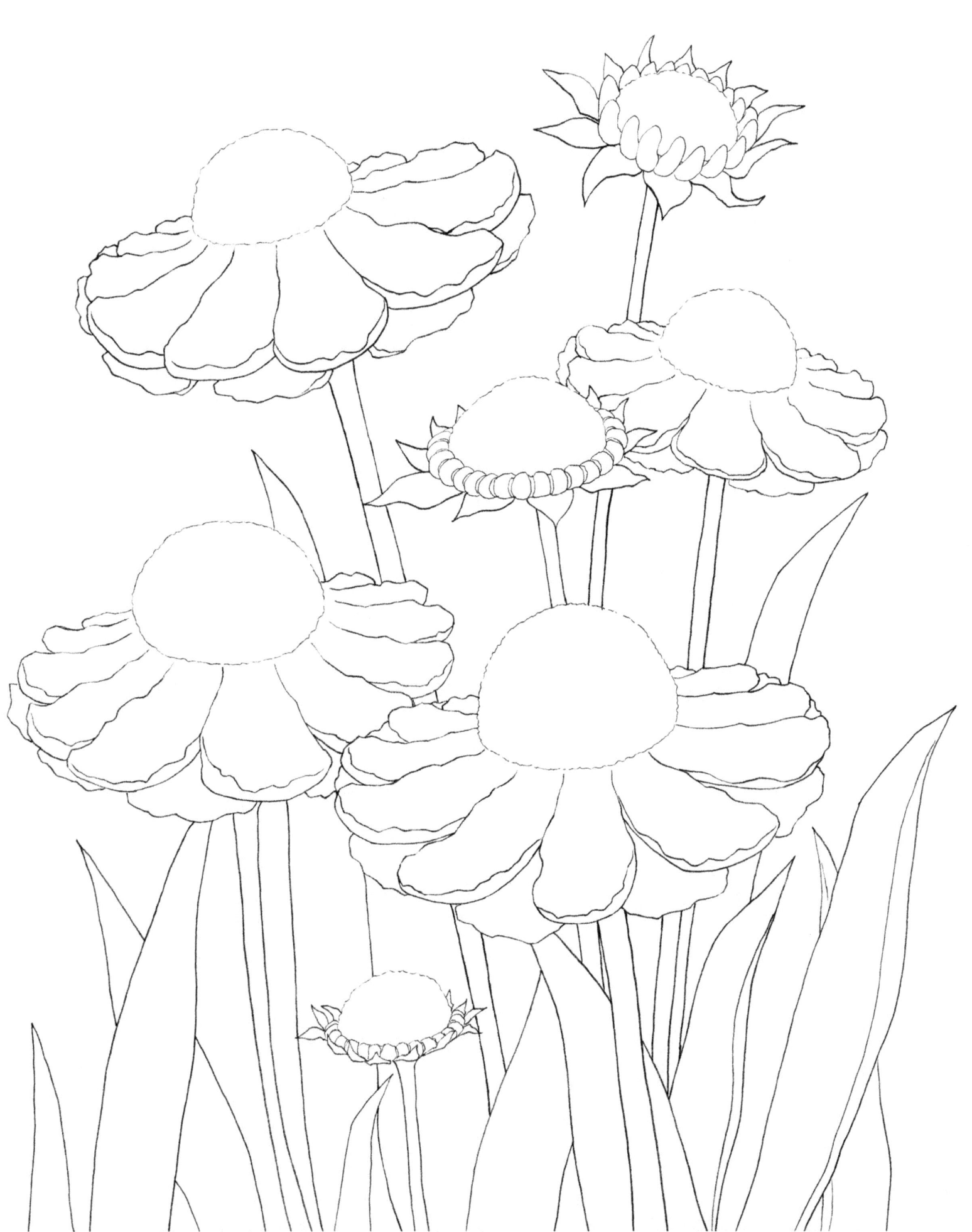

Roses

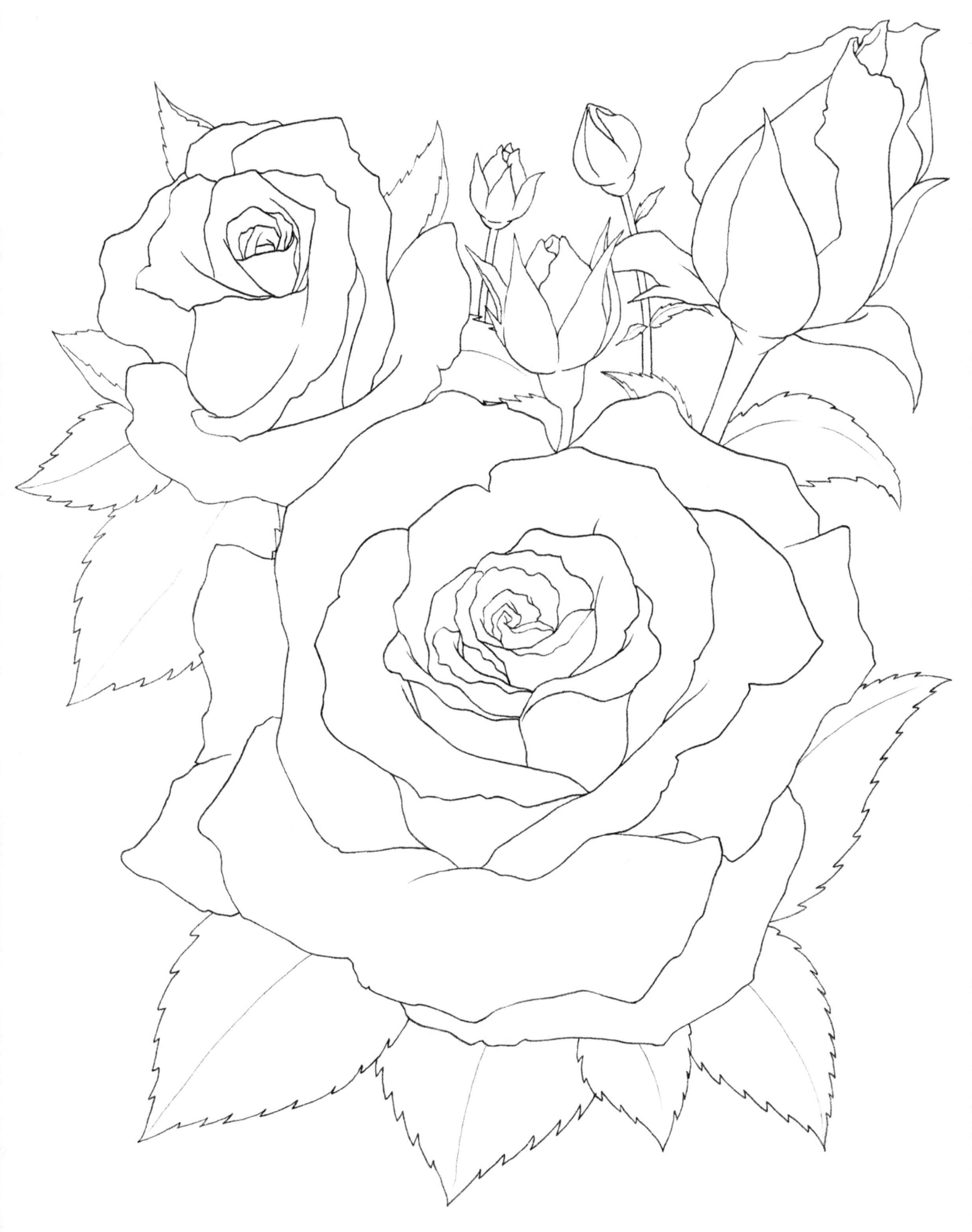

Lily of the Valley

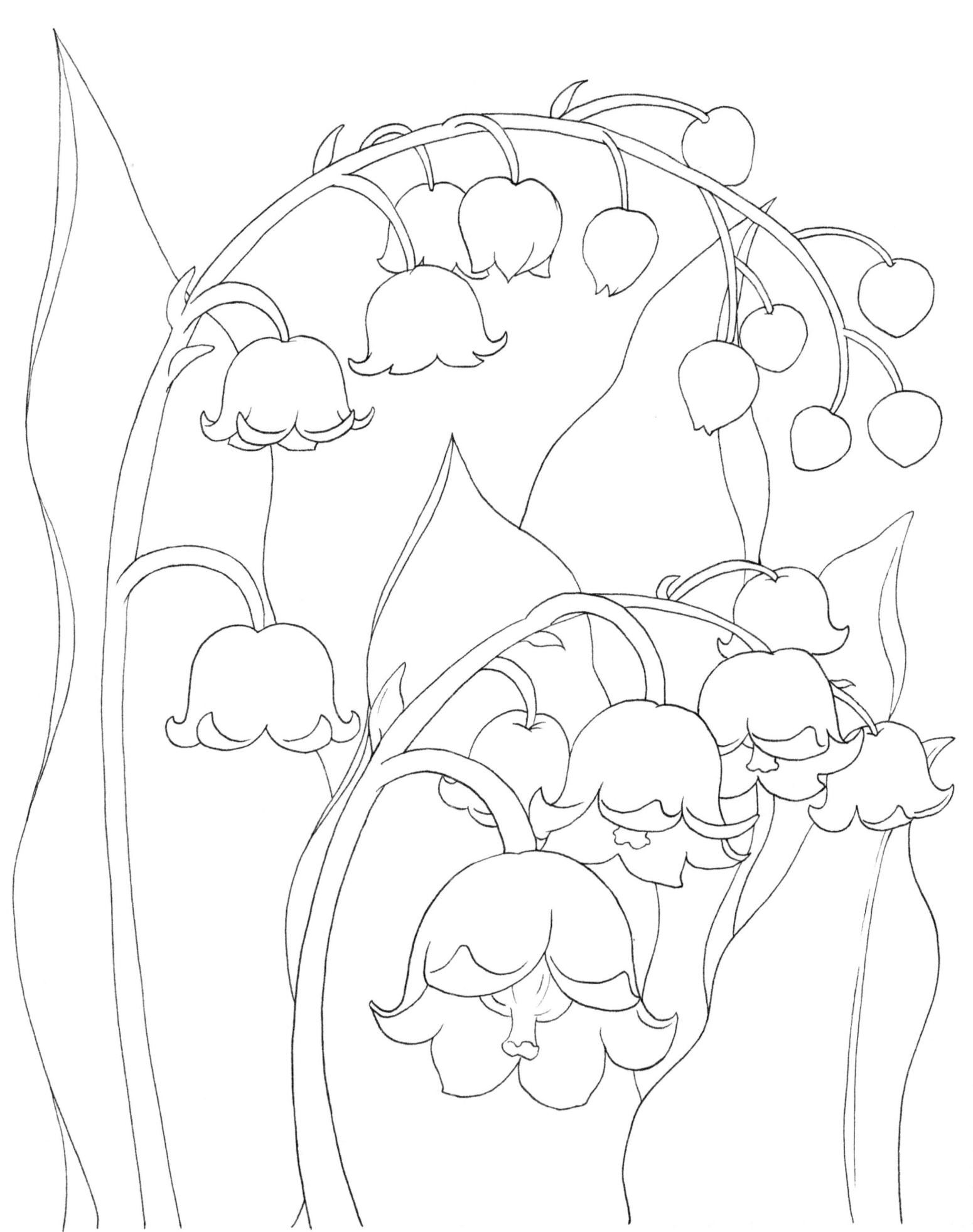

Daisies

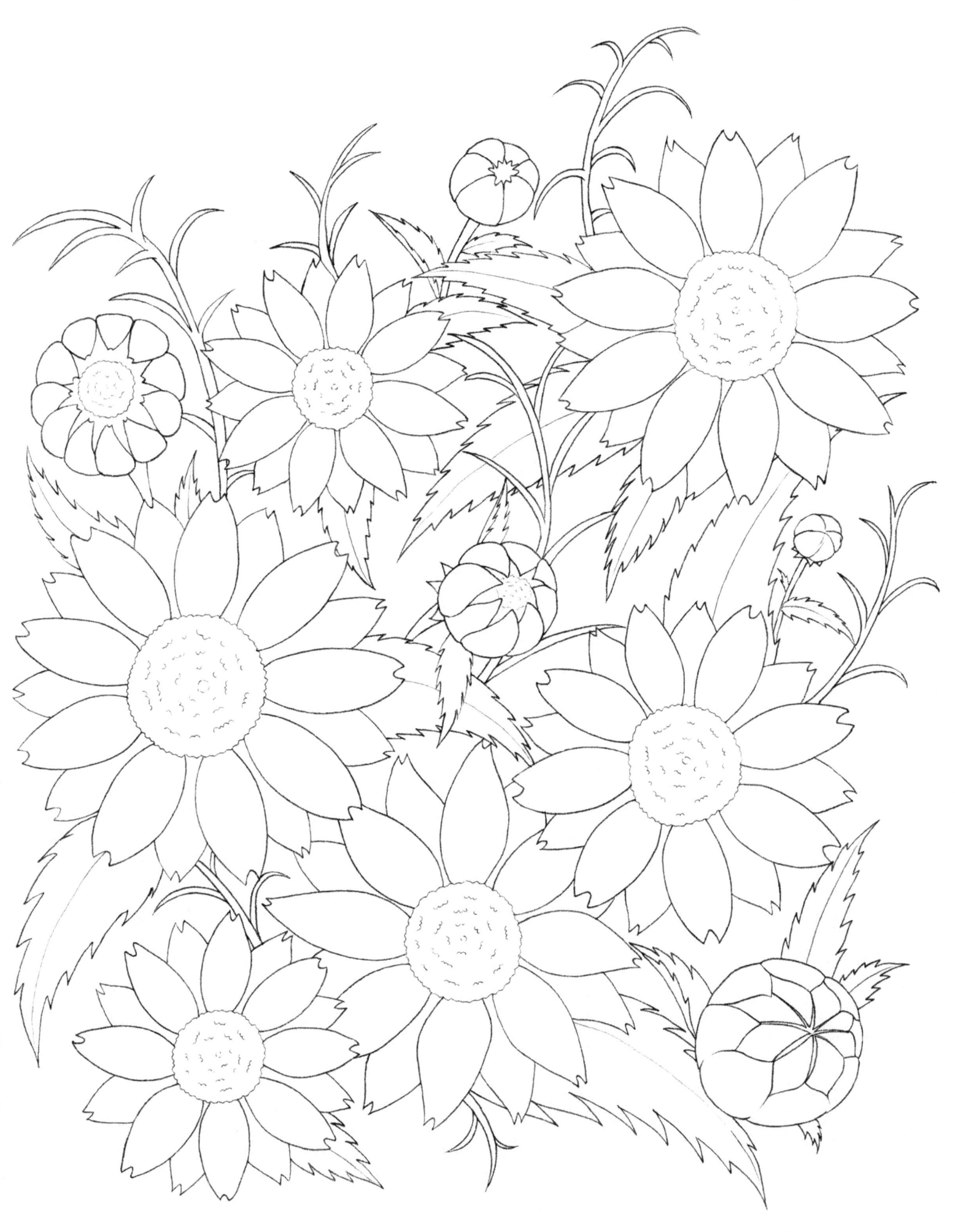

Lavenders

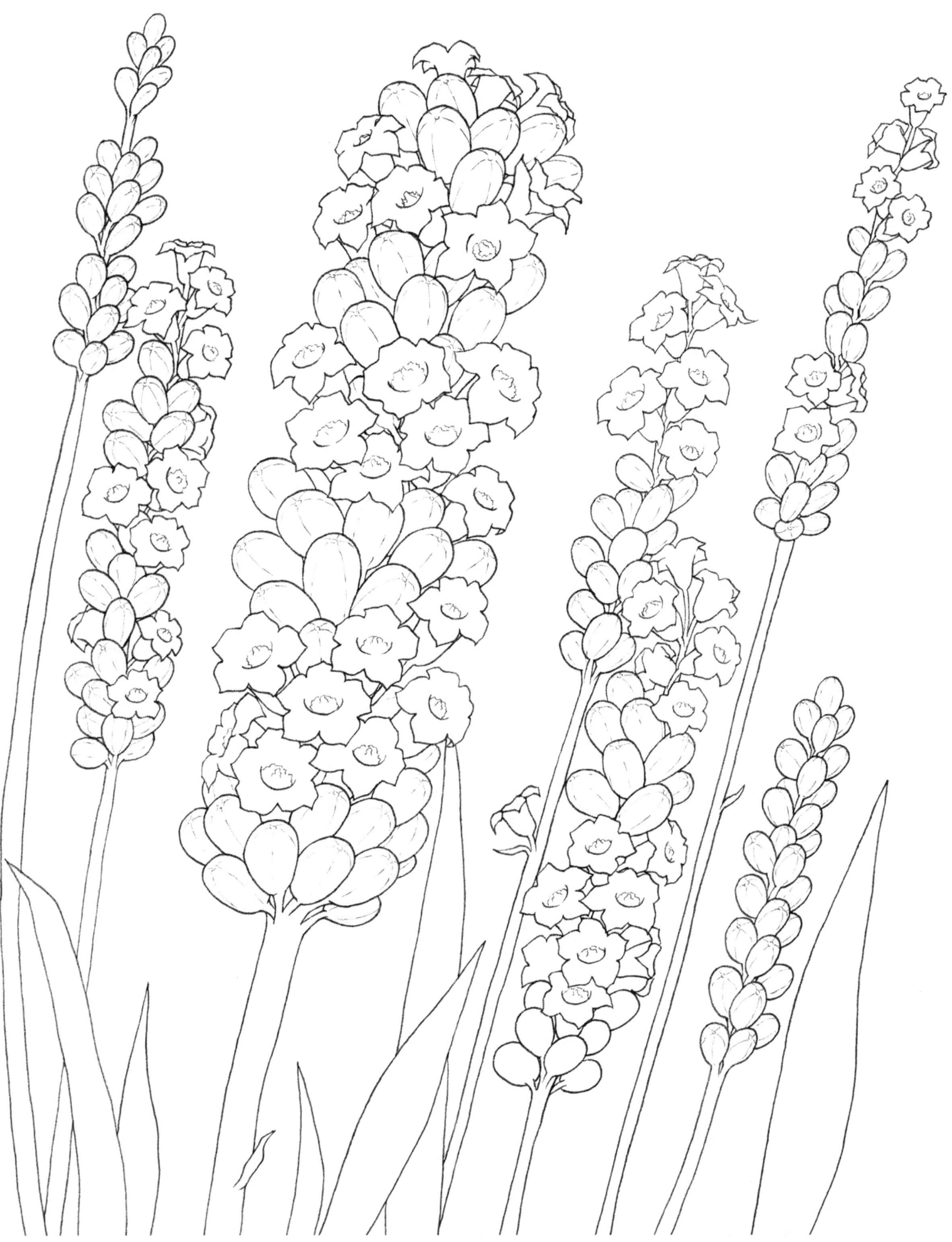

Lilies

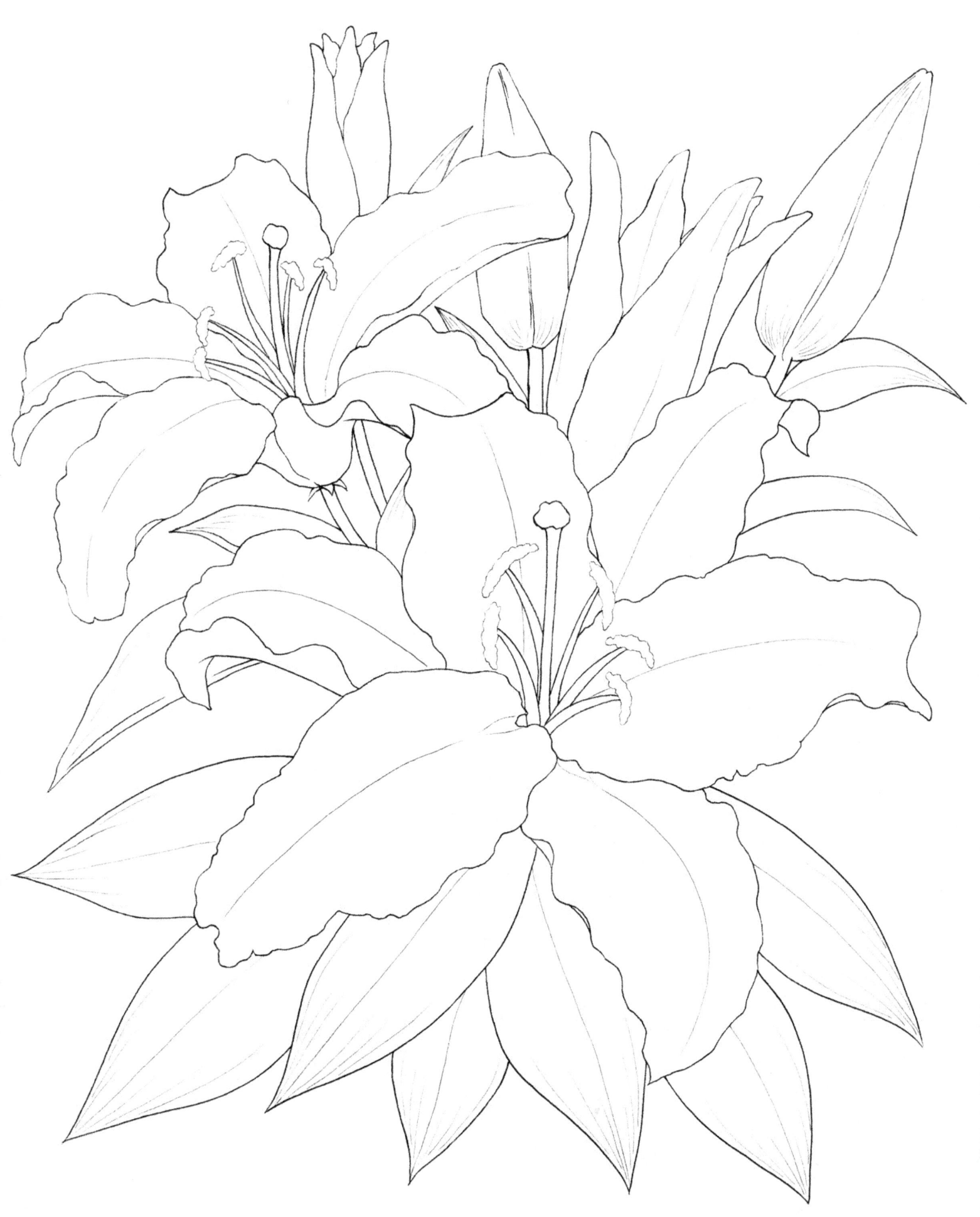

Magnolias

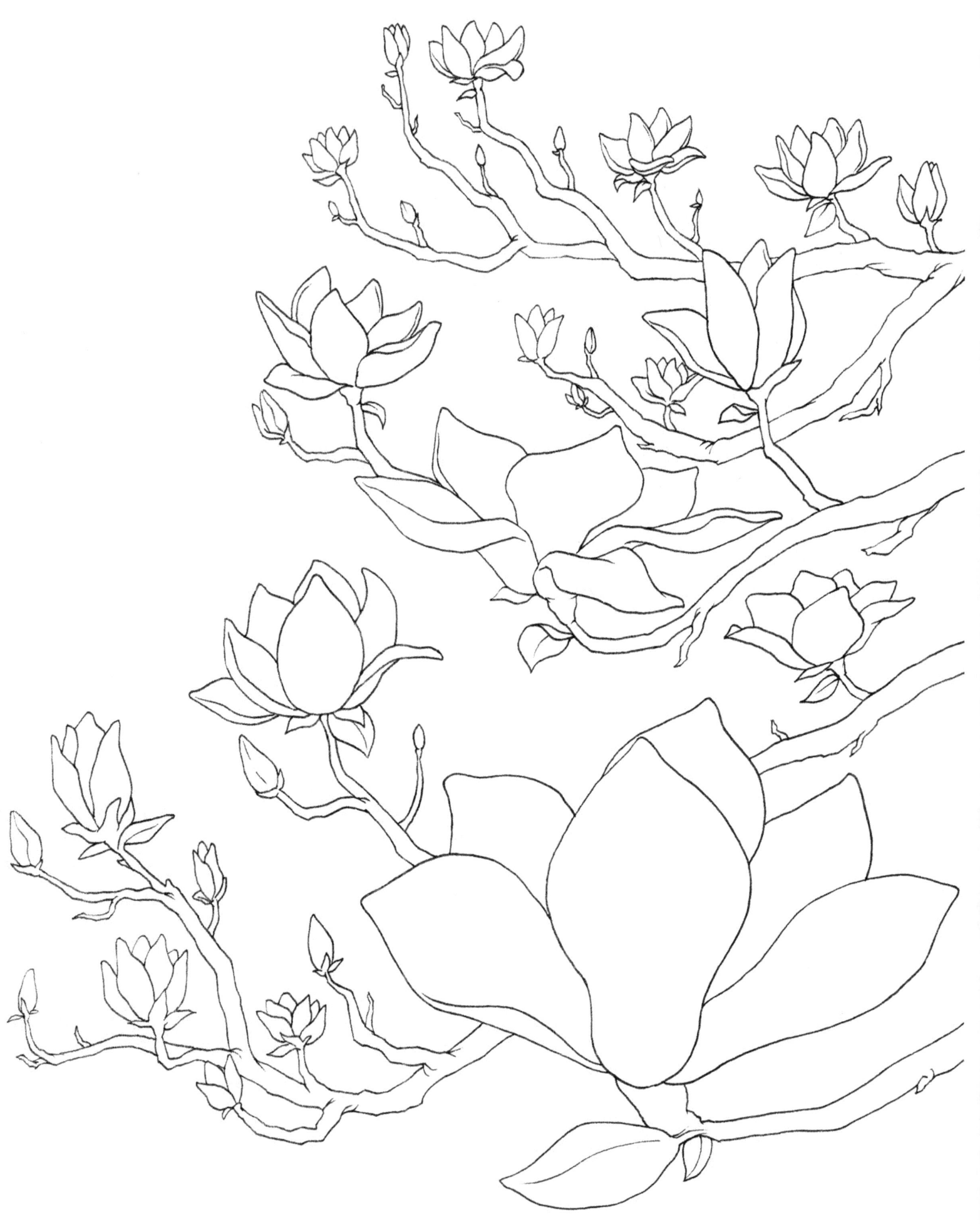

Chrysanthemums

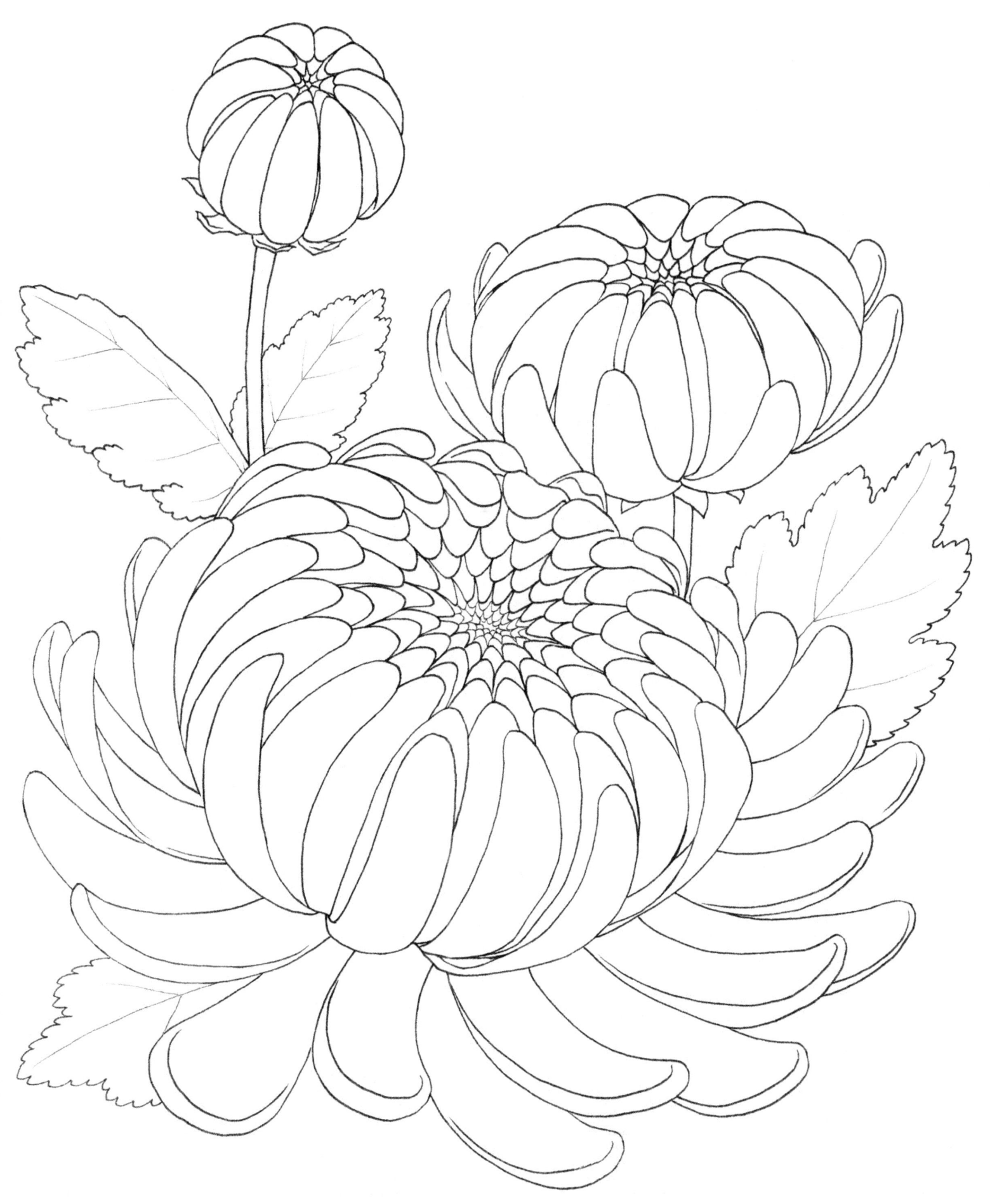

Narcissus flowers

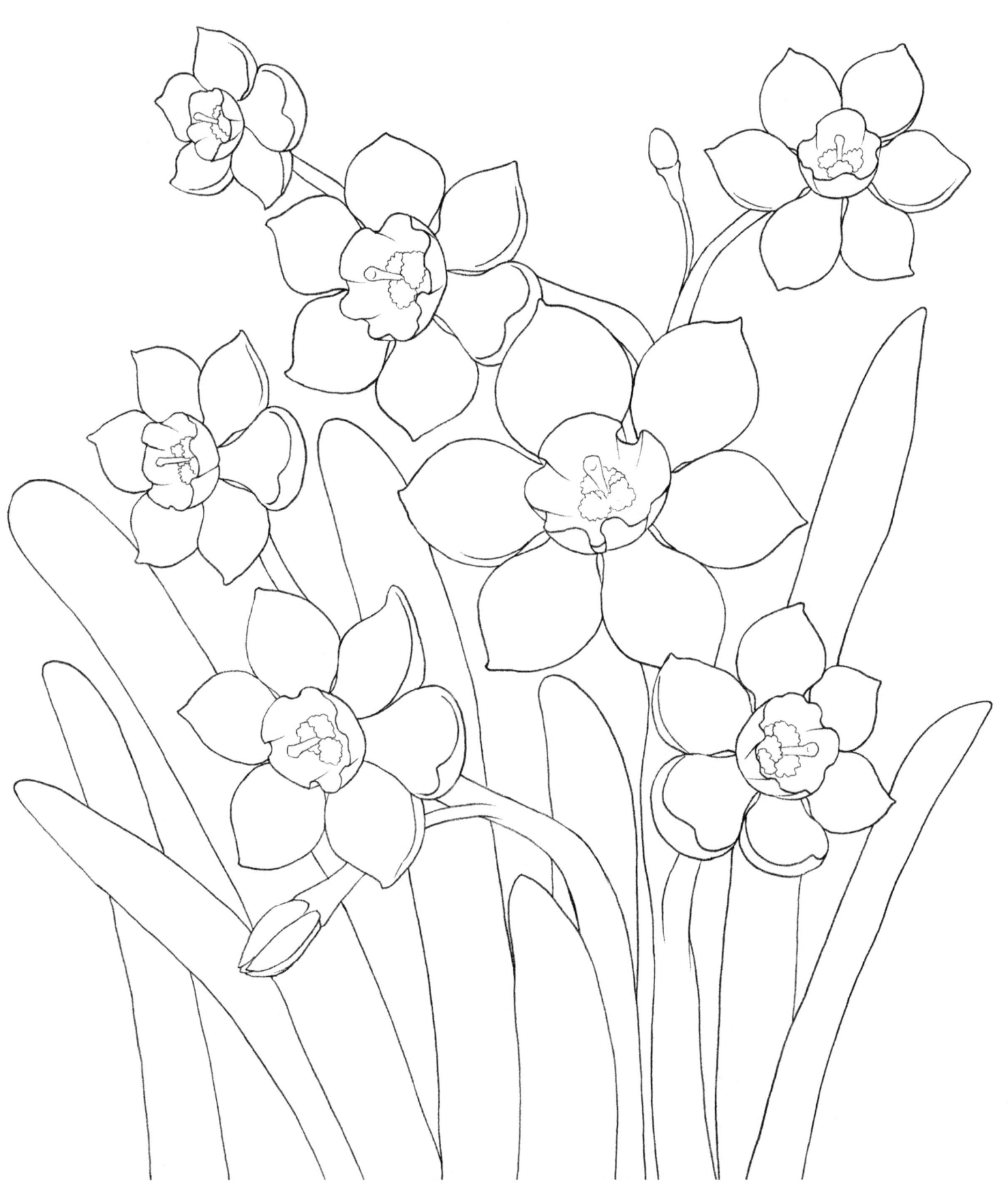

Trumpet flowers

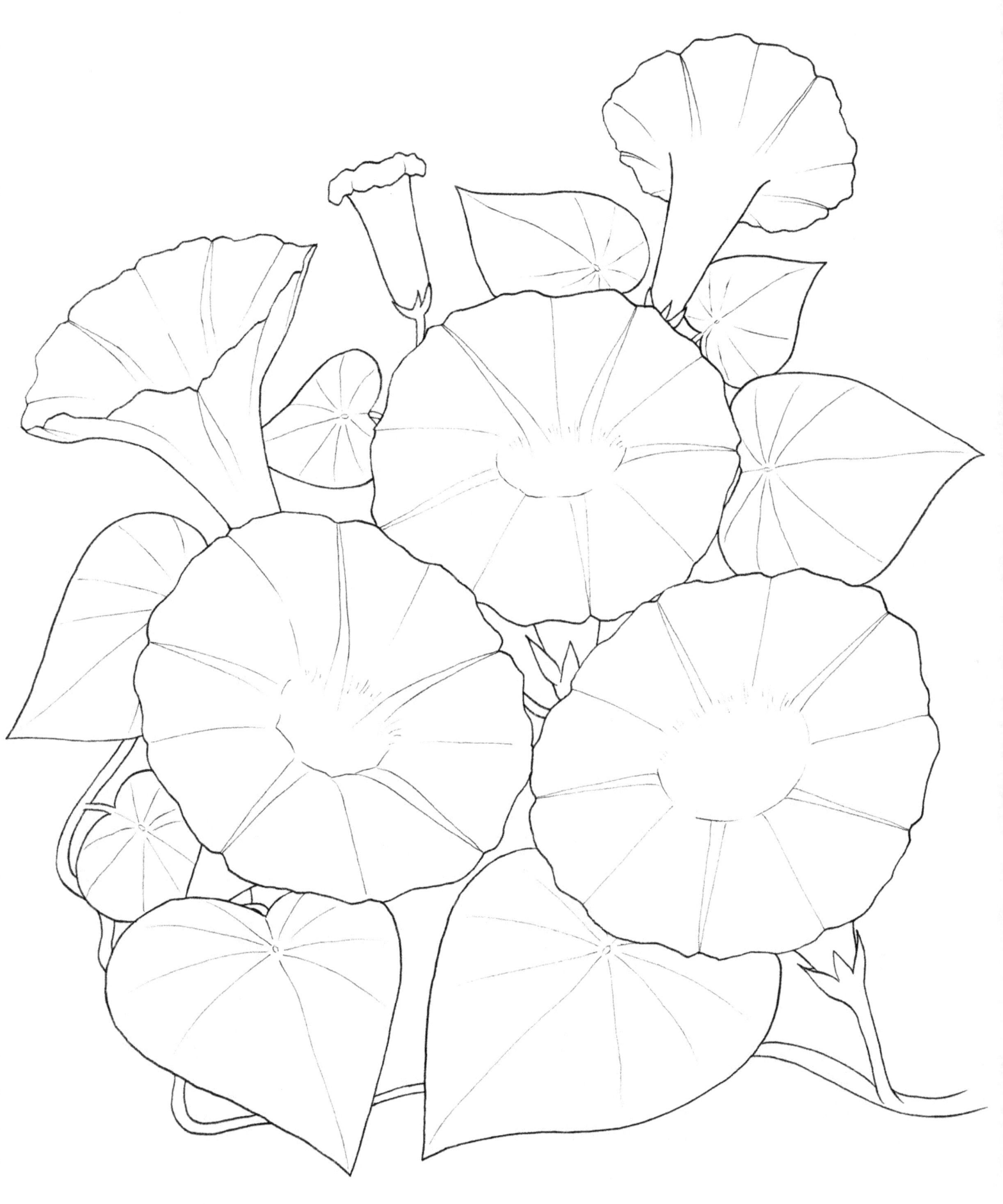

Bauhinias

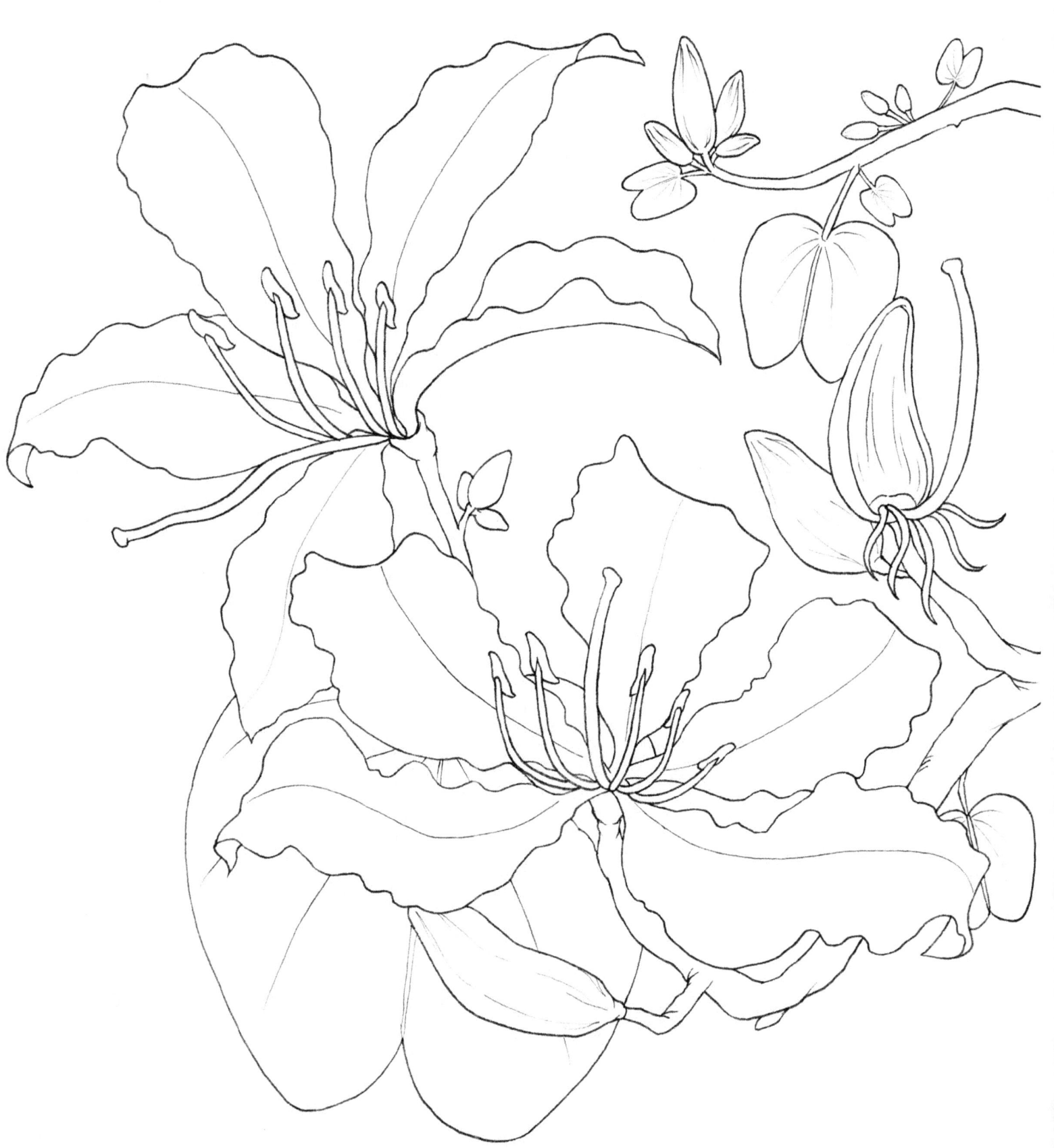

Popies

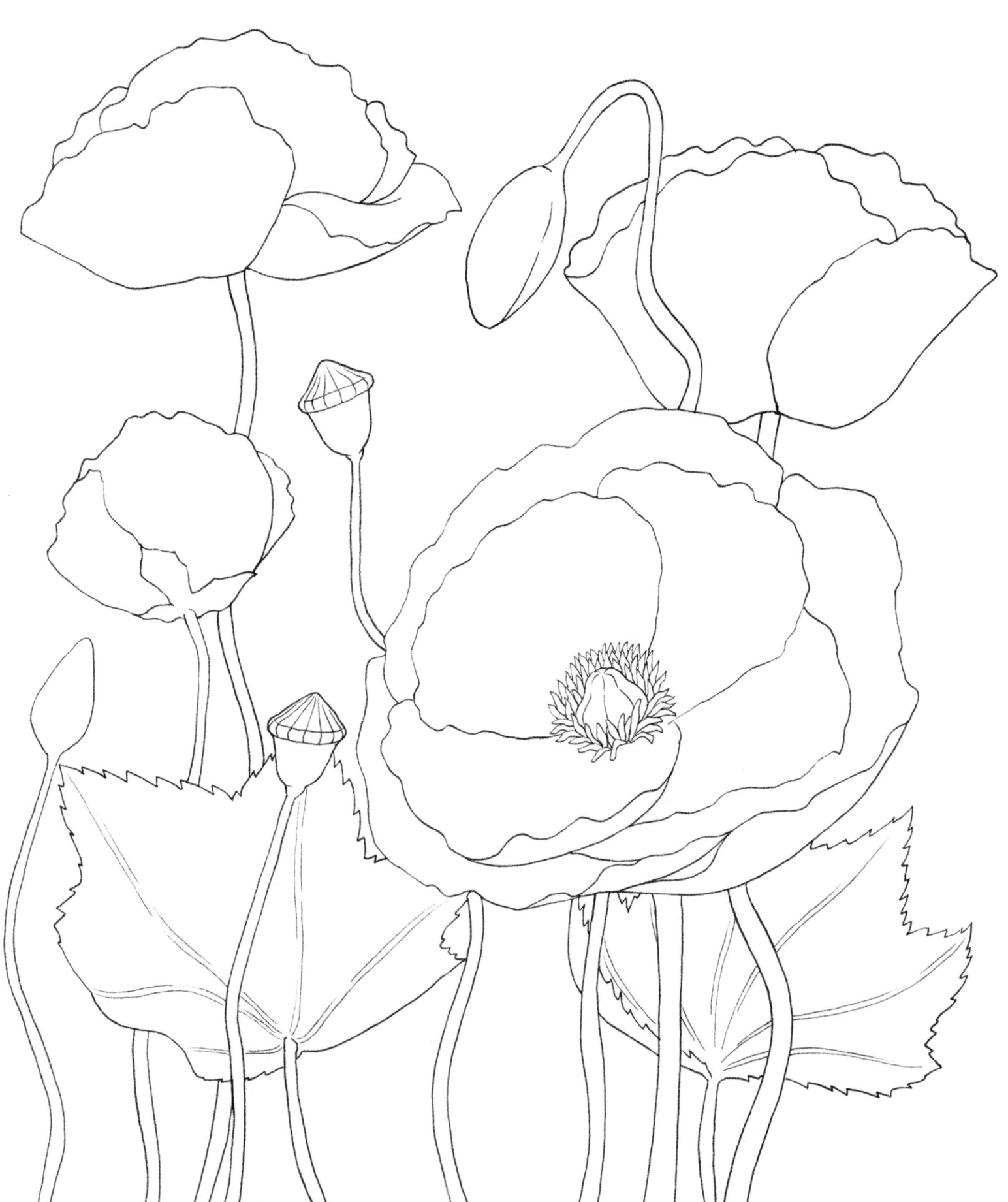

Fuchsia Claudia

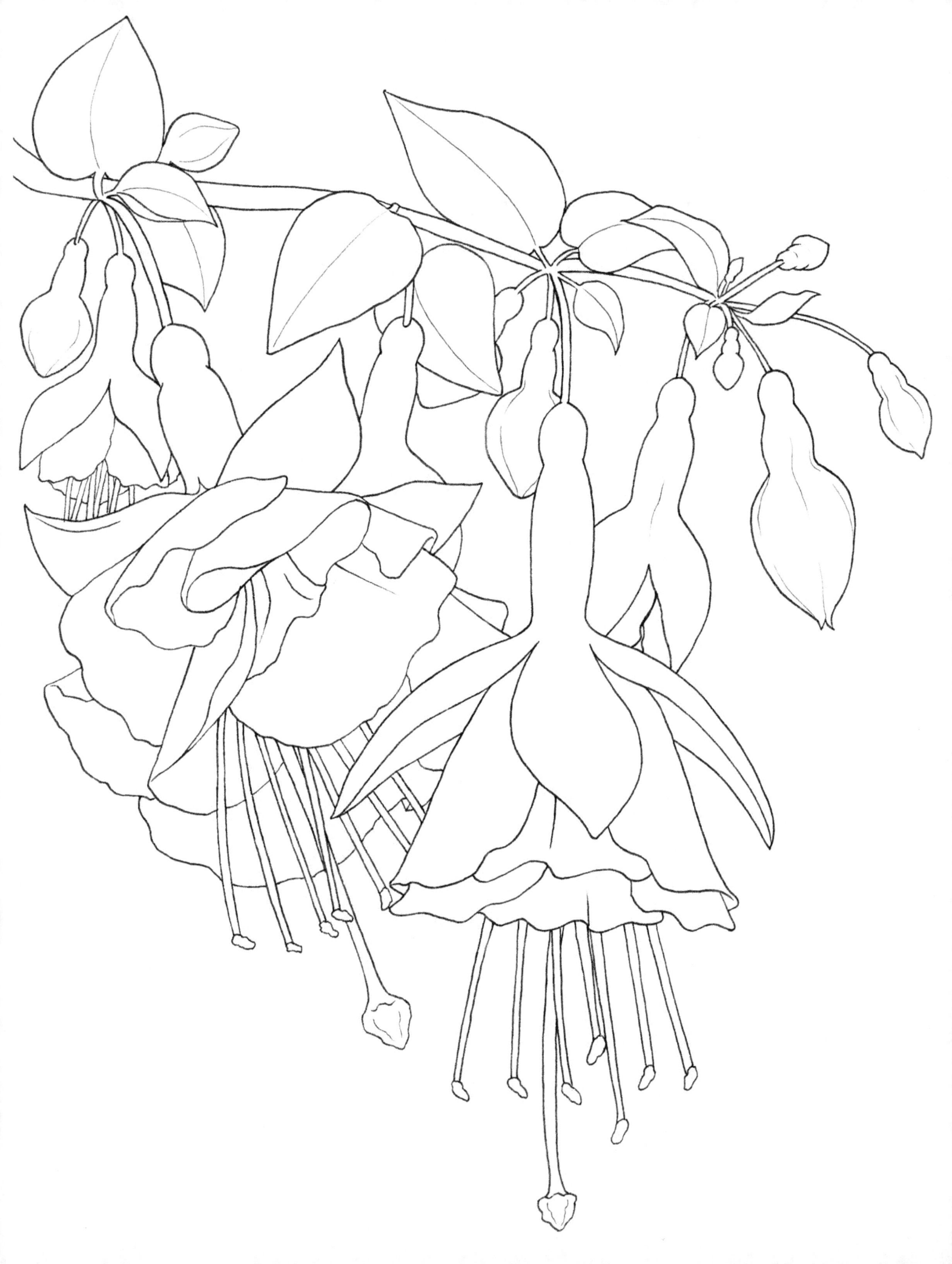

Dahlias

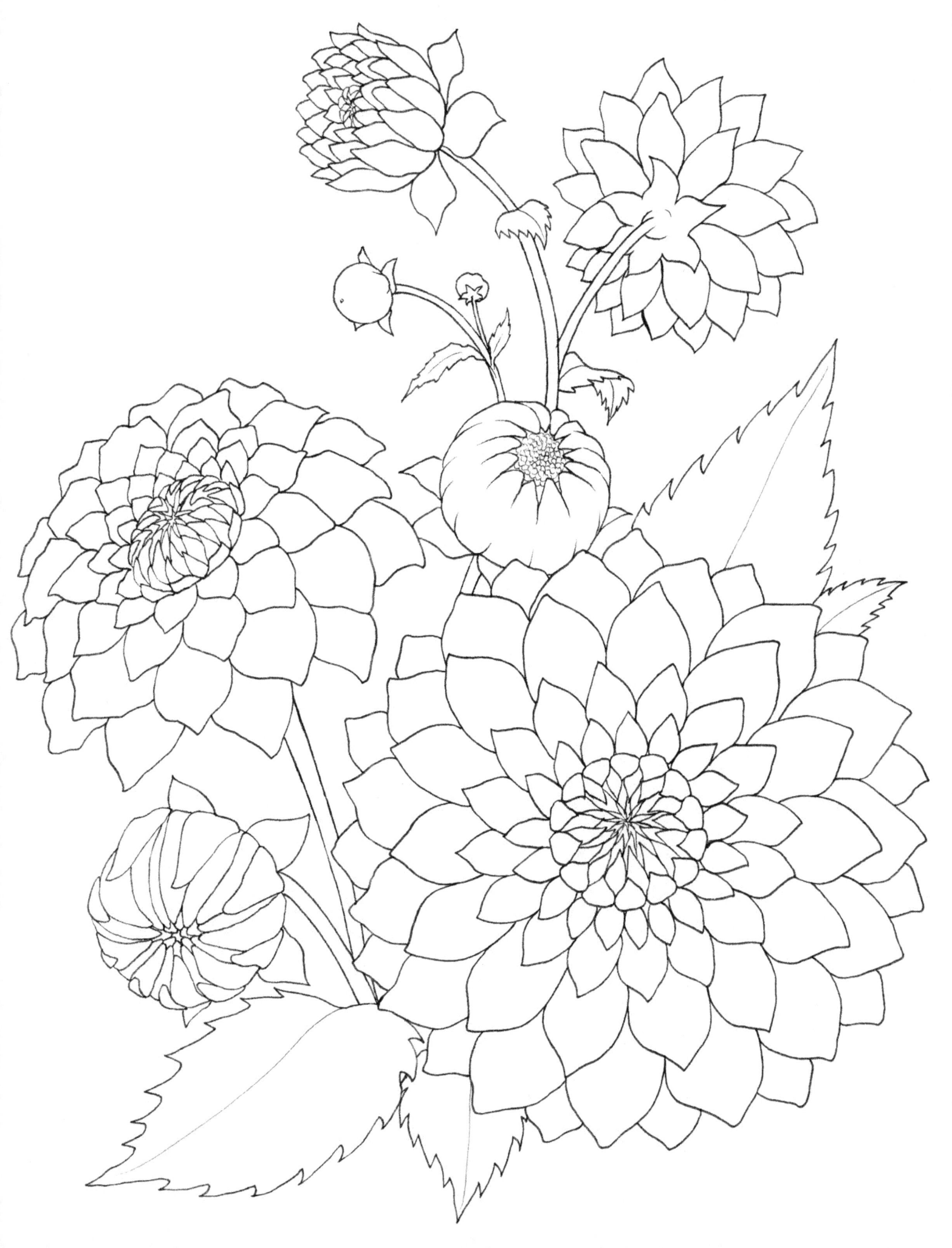

Tulips

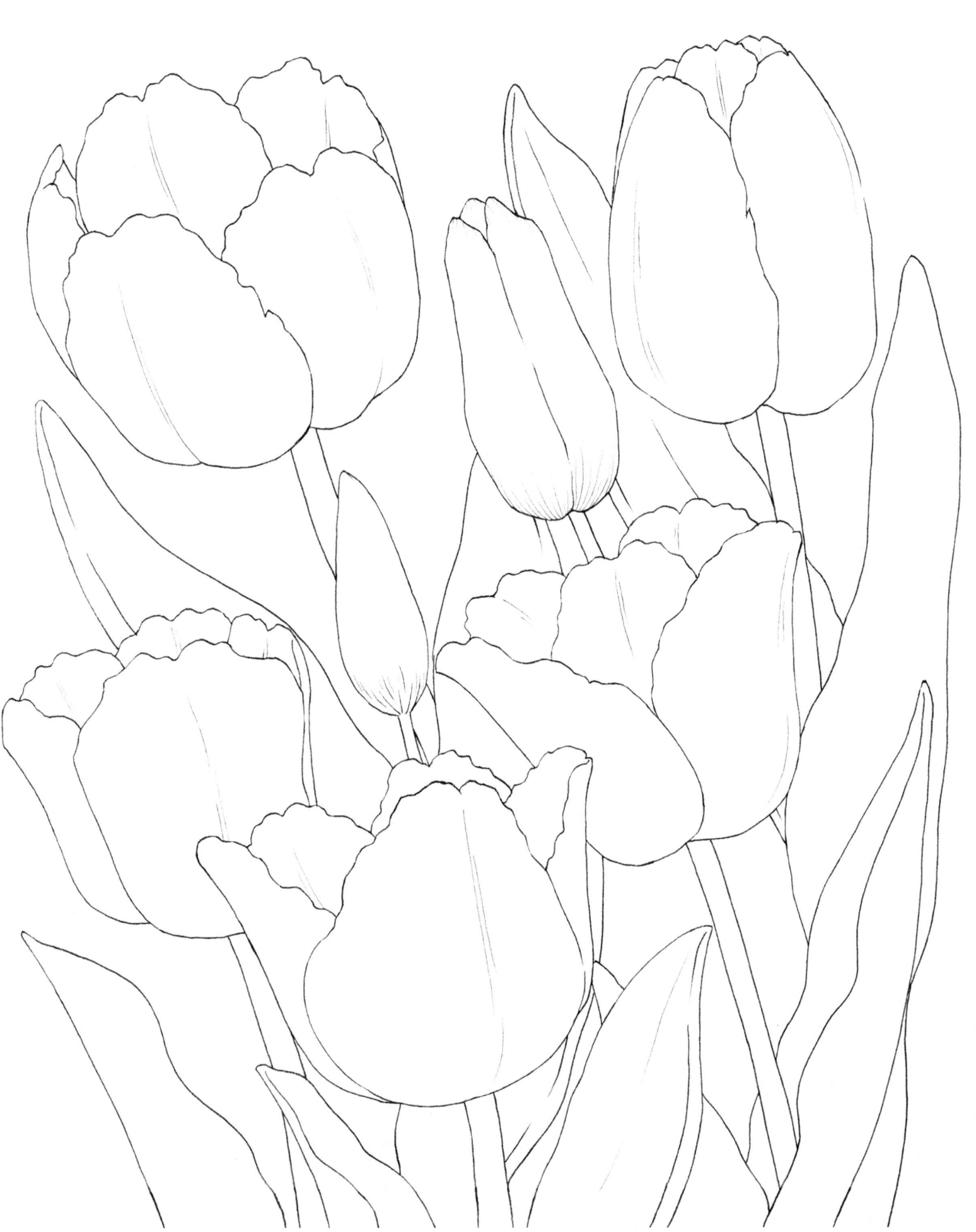

Orchids

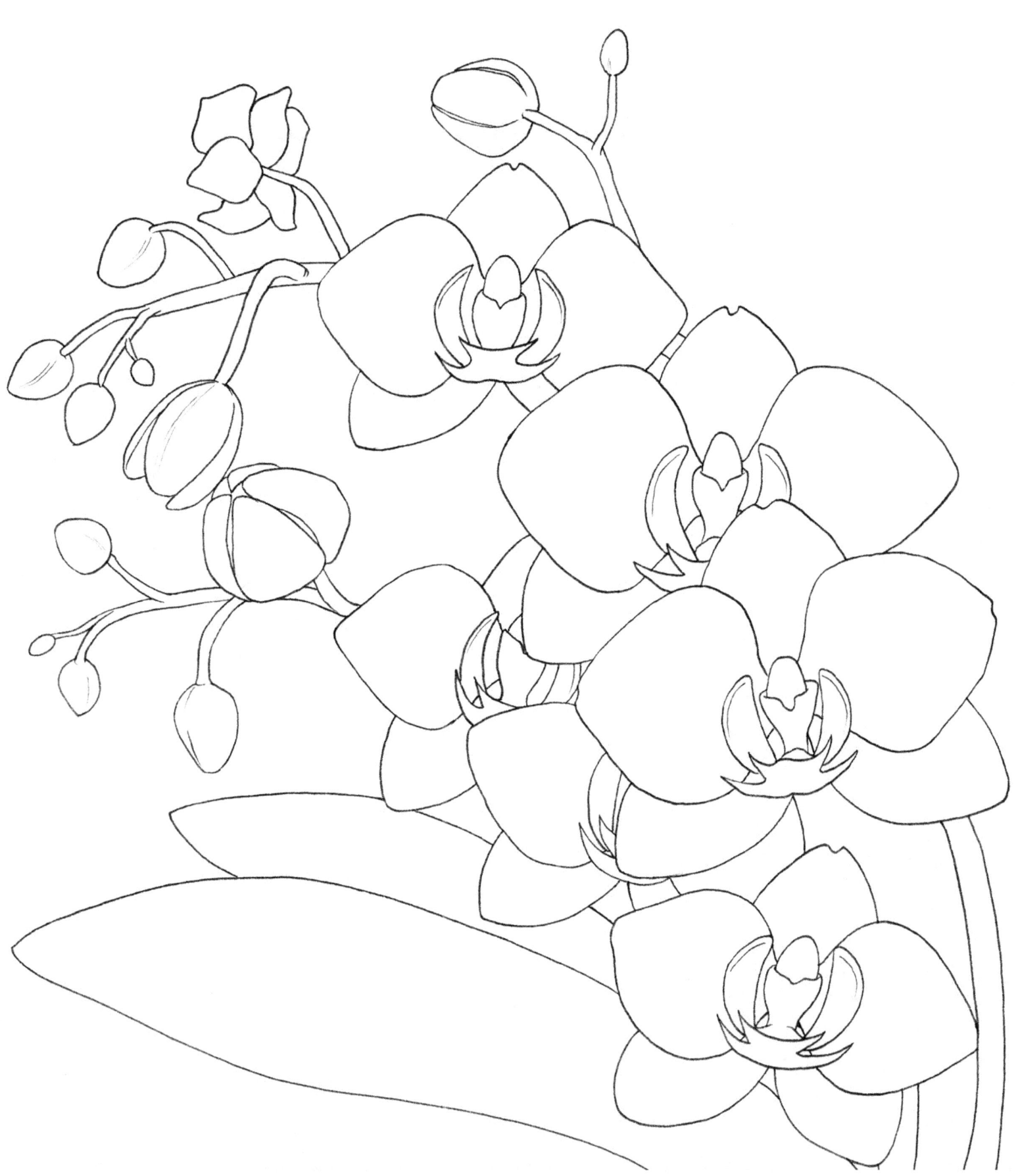

Periwinkles

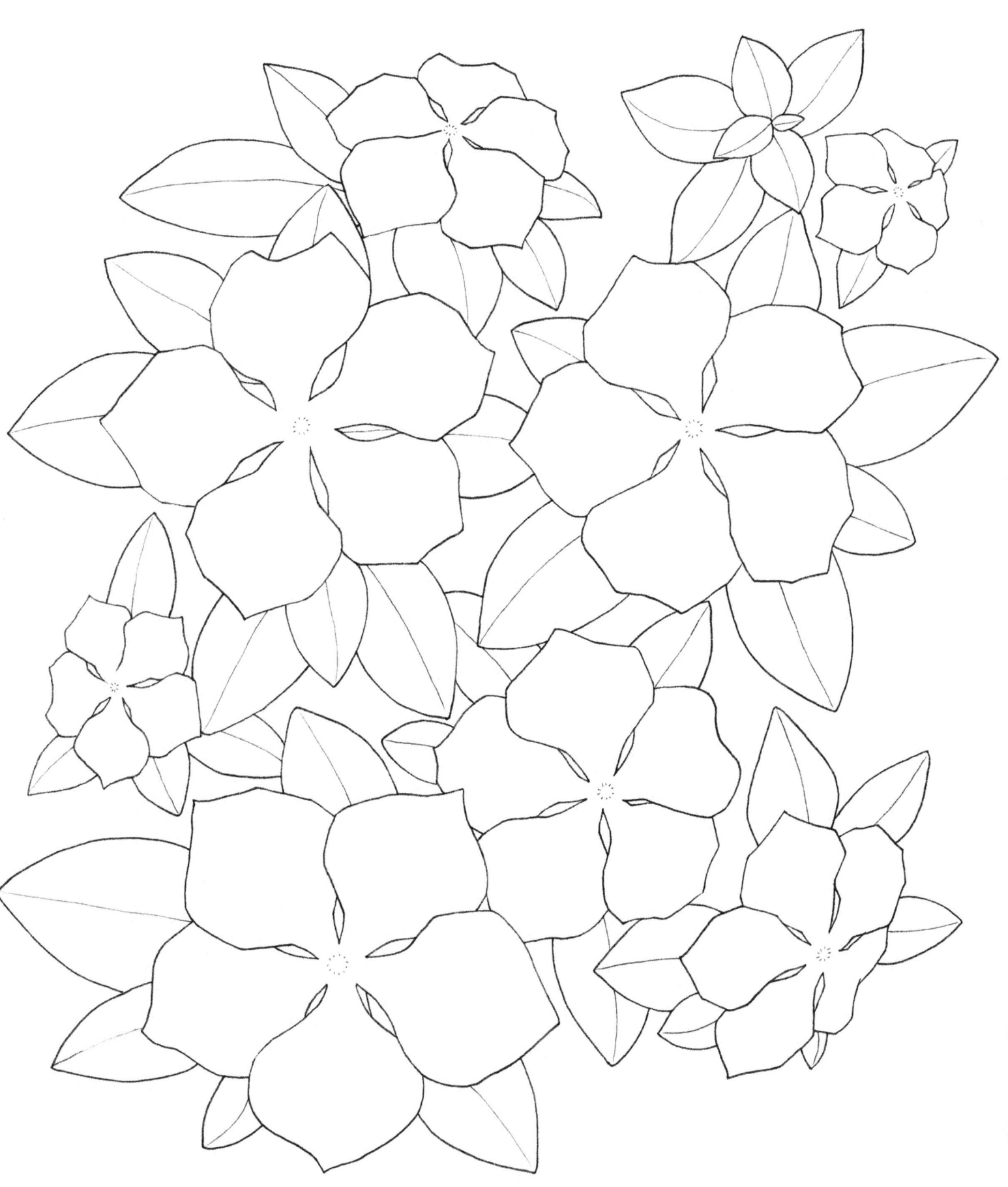

Carnations

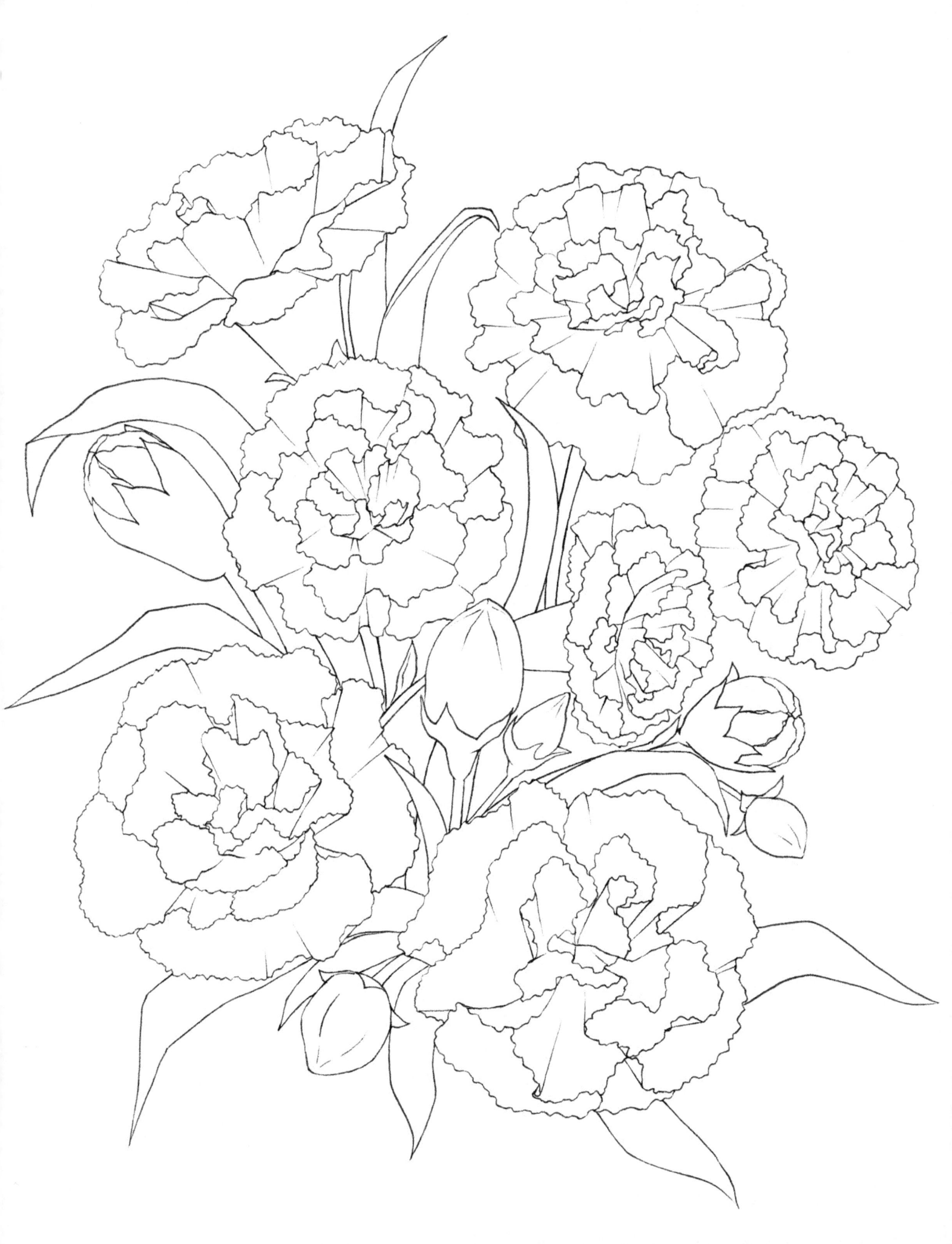

Sunflowers

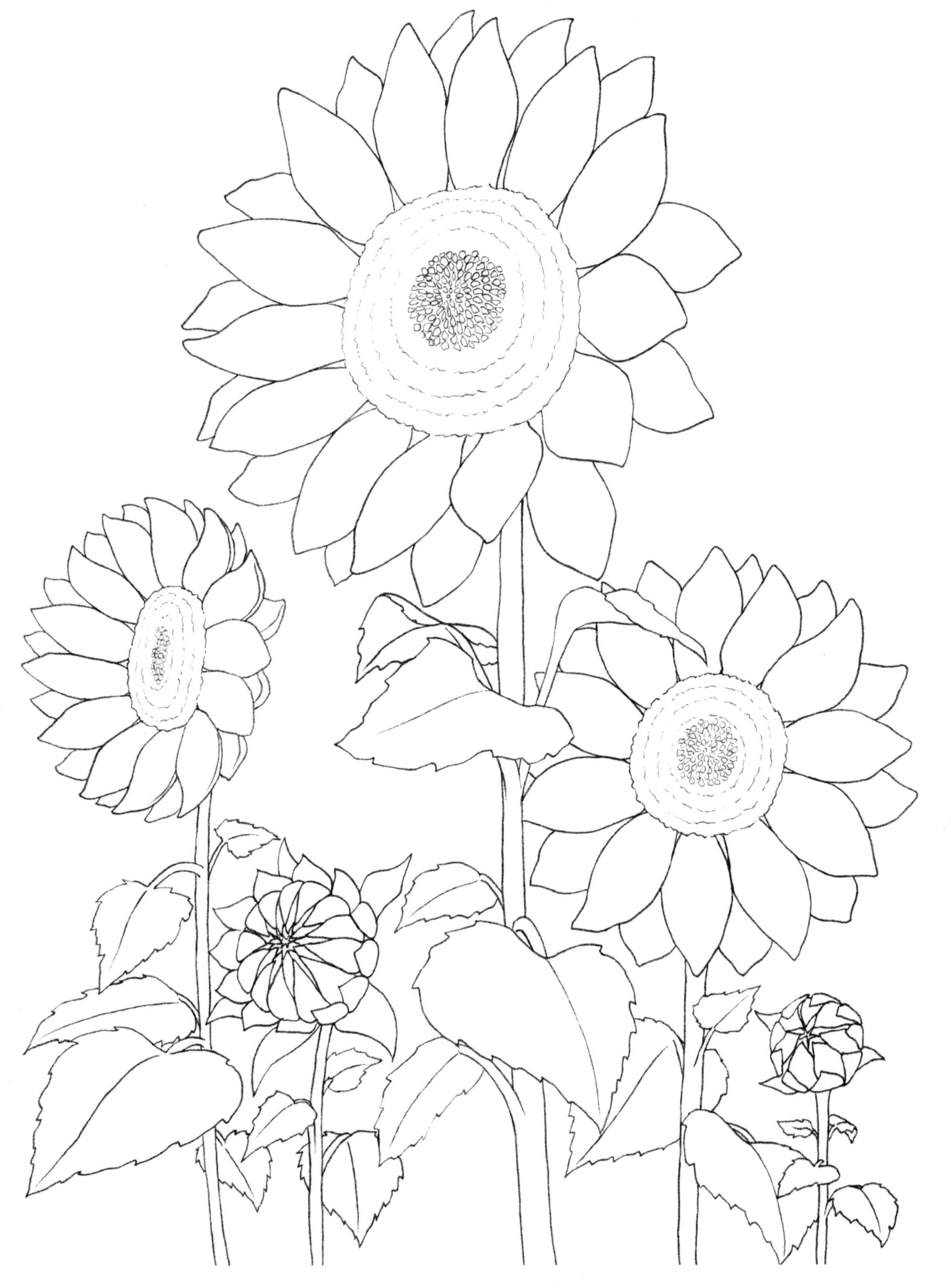